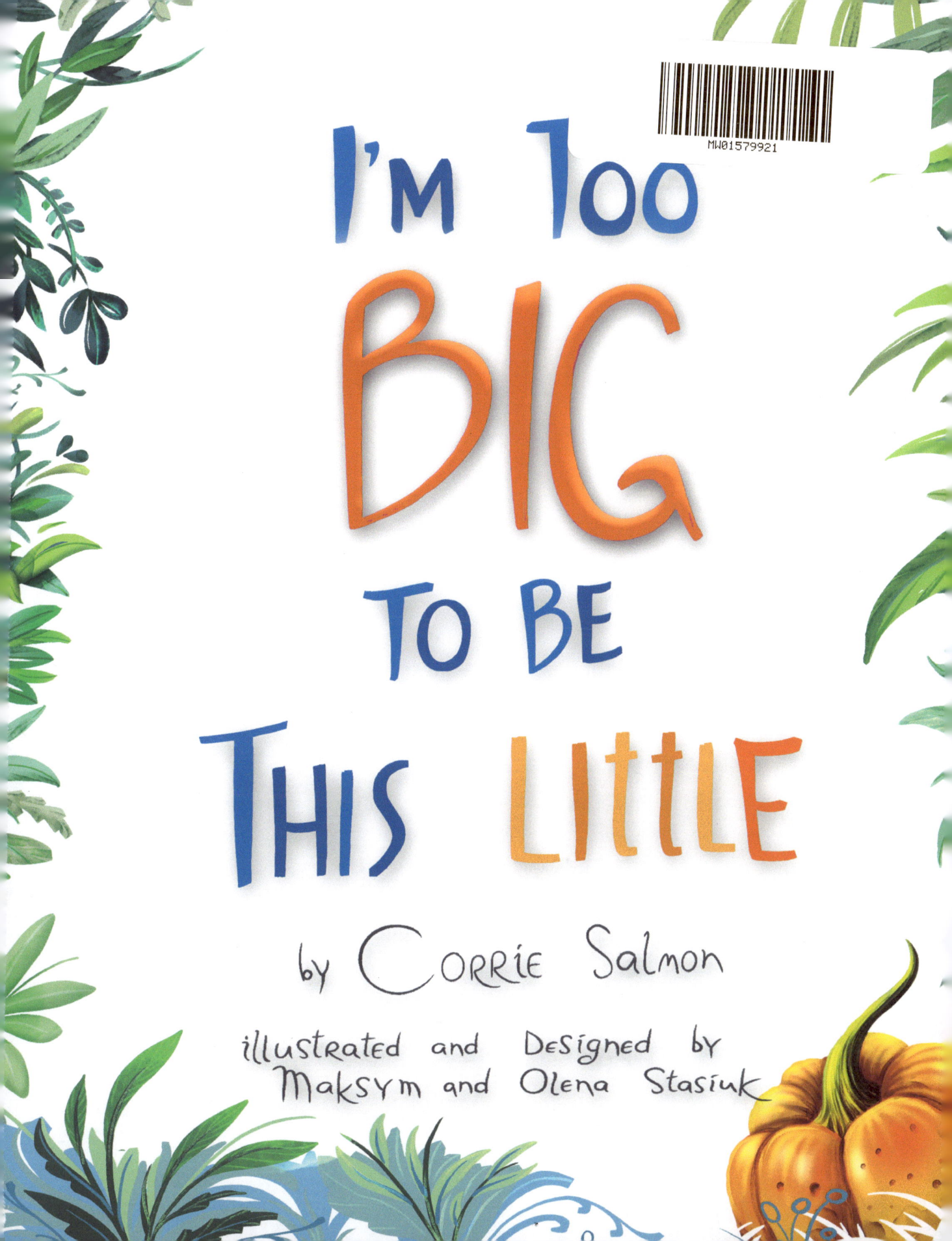

I'm Too BIG to be This Little

by Corrie Salmon

illustrated and designed by Maksym and Olena Stasiuk

To my sweet family -

You are never short on entertaining quips and hilarious perspectives, and you fill my heart with endless love. I love you more than love.

And to Max and Olena,

who showed us just what courage and perseverance really look like.

© 2022 Corrie Salmon. All rights reserved.

No part of this book may be reproduced in any form
without permission from the author, with the exception of short quotations for reviews.
Published by Goose Water Press LLC.

www.kristenemilybehl.com

ISBN:
e-Book: 978-1-954809-03-1
Paperback: 978-1-954809-13-0
Hardcover: 978-1-954809-14-7

Cover design and illustrations by Maksym and Olena Stasiuk.

Mommy says I'm too little to go swimming alone

even though all I need is my orange swimmies and my yellow duckie ring and my flippers and my snorkel and my nose plug and my kickboard and my goggles.

Mommy says I'm too little to drive the car

even though Grandma isn't very much bigger than me and she gets to drive.

Mommy says I'm too little to put makeup on all by myself

even though all I need is red lipstick and bright blue eyeshadow and pink circles on my cheeks and some of that gooey stuff that goes on my eyelashes.

And then I dance around the house singing,

"Allie Allie Grace
with the pretty pretty face!"

And I sing it really loudly because it is obviously everyone's favorite song.

Mommy says I'm too little to carry my own pumpkin when we visit the pumpkin patch
just because I picked out the blue ribbon, gold medal winning,
704-pound pumpkin.
I think Mommy has not felt my muscles lately.

Mommy also says I'm too little to ride the scary rides at the carnival even though I know that if I close my eyes and hang on so tight my knuckles turn white and scream really loud, I'll be fine.

That's what Mommy does.

Mommy says I'm too little to pick out my own clothes for my cousin's wedding even though I look totally fabulous in my polka dot dress with the twirly skirt and my hot pink feather boa and my striped rain boots and my cowboy hat and my sunglasses and Grandma's sparkly purple purse.

Mommy says I'm too little to walk my dog Bella. She's a Great Dane, and I call her Smelly Belly.

Okay, I might actually be too little to walk Bella!

Mommy says I am too big to throw temper tantrums

even though that's the only thing I feel like doing because I'm too little to do anything else.

even though mommy monkeys carry their baby monkeys around all day. Mommy monkeys must be stronger than my daddy.

Mommy says I'm too big to color on the furniture

even though our kitchen table would be much more beautiful if it were lime green with hot pink and purple hearts all over it.

Mommy says that I am too big to fit in my dolly's stroller,

but if I slide in sideways and turn my head to the left and shrug up my shoulders and scrunch up my legs and hold my breath, I fit just fine.

Mommy says that I am too big to throw my food on the floor even though I am only trying to conduct a super-secret scientific experiment to see if peas roll farther than green beans. (Peas win....and I am only sharing this top secret information to save you from getting yourself into trouble.)

Mommy also says I am too big to sleep in Mommy and Daddy's bed with them

even though I know that Daddy is the one who is too big.

One day Mommy asks me why I am so grumpy. So I tell her, "I'm too big to be this little!"

I'm just the right size for hiding in all the really good spots when we play hide-n-go-seek. Mommy can't even fit in the bottom of the coat closet between the vacuum and the snow boots.

I'm just the right size to go down the curvy slide at the park. Mommy tried once, but she got stuck.

Mommy says I'm just the right size to be her kitchen helper. Don't tell her, but the reason her famous chocolate chip cookies are SO famous is because I always throw in a handful of extra chocolate chips when she isn't looking.

I'm just the right size to call Daddy at work and tell him I love him. Mommy says I shouldn't mention how his watch ended up in the potty.

I'm just the right size to ride my trike. You should see my Daddy try and ride it.

His knees come all the way up to his ears!

I am just the right size to go trick-or-treating on Halloween. Maybe this year I will be a cowgirl and Smelly Belly can be my horse.

And at night when I'm really sleepy, I sit on Mommy's lap and lay my head on that comfy spot right between her neck and her shoulder.

And you know what?
I'm just the right size for that, too.

Cookie Recipe by Allie Grace

First, preheat your oven to 375 degrees. This is very important because if you forget, you have to WAIT to bake your cookies. If you have to wait to bake your cookies, you have to wait to EAT your cookies. Nobody is a fan of waiting to eat cookies, so trust me on this one!

Ingredients

- 2 1/4 cups flour
- 1 teaspoon baking soda
- 1 cup butter
- 3/4 cup sugar
- 2 cups semisweet chocolate chips
- 3/4 cup brown sugar
- 2 teaspoons vanilla
- 1/2 teaspoon salt
- 2 large eggs

Instructions

- Stir flour with baking soda and salt; set aside
- In a large bowl, mix softened butter and sugars with a spoon for about 1 minute or until creamy.
- Mix in eggs and vanilla until smooth. Stir in flour mixture just until blended (dough will be stiff). -Stir in chocolate chips. (This is it! Your moment to shine! Quick! Grab an extra handful of chocolate chips and throw those things right on in that mixing bowl!)
- Onto ungreased cookie sheets, drop dough by rounded tablespoonfuls 2 inches apart.
- Bake for 9 to 11 minutes or until light brown. The centers will be soft and the chocolate will be ooey gooey! Cool 2 minutes; remove from cookie sheet to cooling rack. Cool completely.

Store covered in an airtight container (If there are any left. Which there probably won't be. Because YUM!)

About the Author

Corrie Salmon is a Jesus-loving, homeschooling mother of five children. With one already married and four involved in multiple activities in multiple seasons, her family survives in slightly organized chaos and loves every second of it! She and her husband of 22 years are all too familiar with kids becoming TOO big, TOO fast.

About the Illustrators

Maksym and Olena Stasiuk are artists and designers of books, logos, posters and other printing and illustrative products. They live in Ukraine with their two kids, and they design books for clients all over the world. They are crazy about traveling, photography, swimming and snorkeling, drawing and painting, and children's books.
https://www.behance.net/malenax

Don't miss these titles by Goose Water Press!

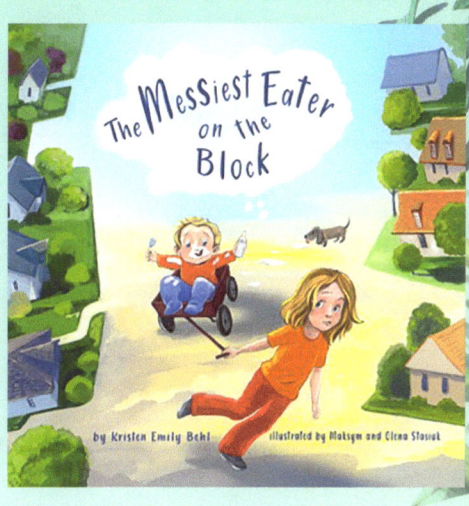

www.kristenemilybehl.com   goose water press   @goosewaterpress

CPSIA information can be obtained
at www.ICGtesting.com
Printed in the USA
LVHW071024110822
725730LV00002B/4